By Dennis R. Shealy

First published by Parragon in 2012
Parragon
Queen Street House
4 Queen Street
Bath BA1 1HE, UK
www.parragon.com

Race Team

A little story for little learners

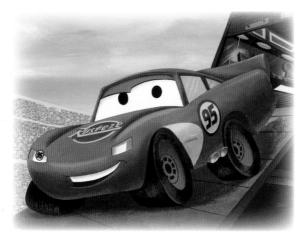

Bath · New York · Singapore · Hong Kong · Cologne · Delhi
Melbourne · Amsterdam · Johannesburg · Auckland · Shenzhen

Lightning McQueen

is going to a race.

Lightning, Mack and the
other cars get ready.

Sarge and Flo bring

cans of gas and oil.

Guido loads Fillmore
with water for Lightning.

The cars drive
to the race.
It is far.

11

Poor Guido gets tired.

Mater gives him a tow.

Big trucks rest
at the truck stop.
The cars keep going.

Mater sees
Lightning and Mack.
There are cars
all around them.

Reporters ask Lightning
about the race.

They take many pictures.

Doc puts on his headset.

It is time for the race.

Mater cheers.
He wants Lightning
to win!

The pit crew is ready.

Lightning drives
to the starting line.
His pit crew yells,
"Go, Lightning, go!"

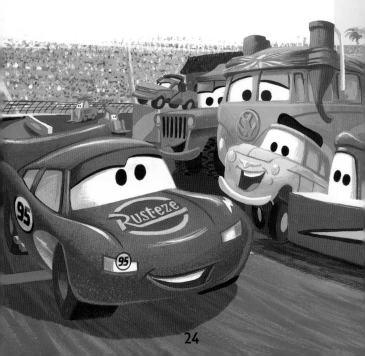

The race starts. Vroom!

Lightning is in front!

He drives the fastest.

Lightning gets tired.

But he keeps going.

Lightning McQueen

wins the race!

Ka-chow!